Michael Fahmy,
Never give up!
Duty, Honor, Country

[signature]
6/11/21

Be inspired!

TANGO
MIKE
MIKE®

THE STORY OF
MASTER SERGEANT
ROY P. BENAVIDEZ

by

YVETTE BENAVIDEZ GARCIA

Photographs taken from the
Benavidez Family Archives

Tango Mike Mike®: The Story of Master Sergeant Roy P. Benavidez
Copyright 2017 by Yvette Benavidez Garcia

Written by Yvette Benavidez Garcia

Photographs taken from the Roy P. Benavidez Family Archives

Requests for permission to make copies of any part of this book should be emailed to the following address:
yvettebgarcia@gmail.com

For more information on Roy P. Benavidez, visit the following sites:

    www.roypbenavidez.wordpress.com
    Facebook: Roy P. Benavidez, "Tango Mike Mike®"
    You Tube: www.youtube.com/roypbenavideztangomikemike
    Twitter: Yvette Benavidez Gar @ RoyPBenavidez
    Instagram: www.instagram.com/roy_p_benavidez
    Pinterest: www.pinterest.com/roypbenavideztangomikemike

DEDICATION

TO MY DAD, Roy. You truly are my hero. You always encouraged me to be the best that I could be, to be myself, and to never let what others say get me down. You always told me, "Yvette, you're OK. The world's wrong." Thank you, Dad. This one's for you.

To Ren, Ryan and Morgan. You've encouraged me every step of the way. Thank you for motivating me, always.

To my mom, Lala. You were always there when Dad couldn't be. Thank you for all of the sacrifices you made. You are an inspiration.

To all those who have daily crosses to carry. Be inspired and believe.

Finally, to the kids who are reading this book. My father dedicated his life to reaching out to those in school. He wanted every child to have the opportunity to finish school and to be the best that they could be. This book is for you. May you be inspired and encouraged to never give up.

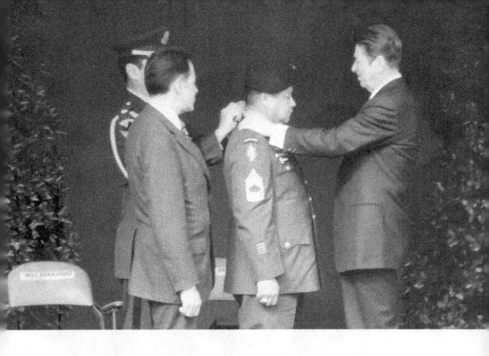

ROY P. BENAVIDEZ is a Medal of Honor recipient from El Campo, Texas. Most people call him a Medal of Honor "Winner," but he never liked that word. If he heard it said, he'd be quick to correct you and say he didn't WIN anything. You see, a winner is someone who wins something, as in a game or a sport. The medal that Roy received, he earned. He fought in a war and received it because he risked his life to save others. He is known among his military brothers as "Tango Mike Mike." The US military uses certain words to designate as call signs. "Tango Mike Mike," a nickname given to Roy by his brothers-in-arms, would translate into "That Mean Mexican." Although Roy was anything but mean. Roy was a soldier who went above and beyond the call of duty and voluntarily risked his life to retrieve classified documents and save the lives of others. His tenacious attitude, unstoppable drive and unyielding desire to save his comrades earned him the call sign, "Tango Mike Mike."

ROY WAS BORN on August 5, 1935, in a rural South Texas town named Lindenau. He and his younger brother, Roger, were born during a time when there was segregation and racism. Roy hated the fact that some people looked at the color of someone's skin, instead of red, white and blue — the colors of the American flag.

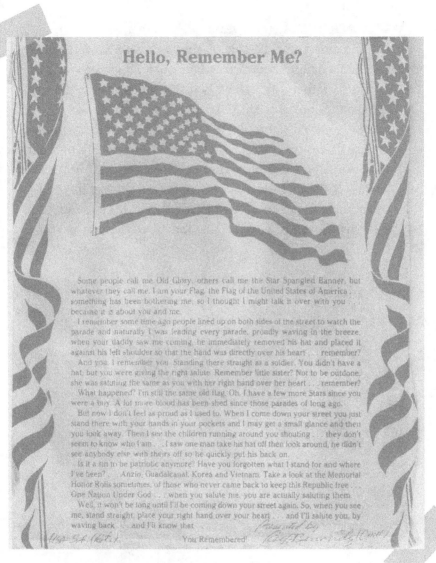

Hello, Remember Me?

Some people call me Old Glory, others call me the Star Spangled Banner, but whatever they call me, I am your Flag, the Flag of the United States of America... something has been bothering me, so I thought I might talk it over with you... because it is about you and me.

I remember some time ago people lined up on both sides of the street to watch the parade and naturally I was leading every parade, proudly waving in the breeze, when your daddy saw me coming, he immediately removed his hat and placed it against his left shoulder so that the hand was directly over his heart... remember?

And you, I remember you. Standing there straight as a soldier. You didn't have a hat, but you were giving the right salute. Remember little sister? Not to be outdone, she was saluting the same as you with her right hand over her heart... remember?

What happened? I'm still the same old flag. Oh, I have a few more Stars since you were a boy. A lot more blood has been shed since those parades of long ago.

But now I don't feel as proud as I used to. When I come down your street you just stand there with your hands in your pockets and I may get a small glance and then you look away. Then I see the children running around you shouting... they don't seem to know who I am... I saw one man take his hat off then look around, he didn't see anybody else with theirs off so he quickly put his back on.

Is it a sin to be patriotic anymore? Have you forgotten what I stand for and where I've been?... Anzio, Guadalcanal, Korea and Vietnam. Take a look at the Memorial Honor Rolls sometimes, of those who never came back to keep this Republic free... One Nation Under God... when you salute me, you are actually saluting them.

Well, it won't be long until I'll be coming down your street again. So, when you see me, stand straight, place your right hand over your heart... and I'll salute you, by waving back... and I'll know that...

You Remembered!

This was Roy's favorite poem. He had it memorized word for word and often ended his speeches with it. (Author unknown)

WHEN ROY WAS three years old, his father, Salvador Jr., got sick and died from tuberculosis. His mother, Teresa, remarried and had a daughter named Lupe. Four years later, she gave birth to another girl, named Bellatres, but she passed away at only six months of age. On September 25, 1946, when Roy was only eleven years old, his mother died from the same disease that took his father's life. This left Roy and his brother orphans. After the death of both of his parents, Roy's uncle, Nicolas Benavidez, offered to raise the two boys. His young sister, Lupe, stayed behind with her father. Roy's uncle moved the two boys to El Campo, Texas, and raised them as his own.

From left to right are Roy's uncle Nicolas and aunt Alexandria Benavidez, along with Roy and his wife, Lala, at their wedding reception. To the right are Lala's parents, Maria Hansen and Juan Coy. June 7, 1959.

This was the only picture Roy had of his mother, Teresa Perez Benavidez.

This photo, of Roy's parents (Salvador and Teresa Perez Benavidez) on their wedding day, was found in the Benavidez Family Archives after Roy had passed away. Unfortunately, Roy never got to see it.

YOUNG ROY HAD to earn his keep while living with his new family. He had nine new brothers and sisters, and life was not easy. Not only did he have to deal with the death of both of his parents, he now had to learn to live with and love a new family.

Roy earned extra money shining shoes, selling his aunt Alexandria's tacos, and helping the family pick cotton. He and his new brothers and sisters also spent their summers working in the fields and putting aside the little money that they made to help their parents.

ROY'S HARDSHIPS CONTINUED as a child. In fact, he left his hometown so often to pick cotton that he had to drop out of school. He was not proud of this, but at the time, he did not have a choice. Later in life, Roy would say in his speeches … "Like a fool, I dropped out of school." He always regretted this circumstance.

Growing up, Roy was not the perfect kid. He got into trouble a lot and he took to boxing to let out his frustrations. His uncle Nicolas spent many days at the school principal's office dealing with Roy's behavior.

Roy's uncle, Nicolas Benavidez, who raised and loved Roy as his own.

Roy at the age of fourteen.

THE RACISM AND segregation that Roy experienced didn't help his fighting attitude. It actually fueled the fire that was in Roy. There were times when Roy couldn't watch a movie in the local theater or sit in any seat that he wanted. There were signs that instructed all Blacks and Mexicans to go around and enter through the back and to sit up in the balcony. Similarly, restaurants had signs that said, "No Blacks or Mexicans allowed." Situations like this made Roy feel as if he wasn't worthy, but he never let that get him down. In fact, it was because of this that he wanted to better himself and make his aunt and uncle proud of him.

Sicily Drop Zone. Roy captioned this picture "Me coming in for a PLF," which stood for "Parachute Landing Fall."

Fort Benning, Georgia, Training Facility. This is where Roy trained to become a paratrooper.

IN 1952, WHEN Roy turned seventeen years old, he decided to join the Texas National Guard. This was his way of doing something good with his life. He believed that if he joined the military he could earn a better education and be trained for combat operations. He stayed in the Texas National Guard for three years. His real desire, however, was to join the Army and become a Green Beret.

EARLY IN HIS military career, Roy met a young, green-eyed Irish girl named Hilaria Coy. He affectionately called her "Lala" and began courting her. Lala's parents were very strict and did not allow Lala to see Roy without the supervision of her older brothers. Every time Roy wanted to take her out, one of her brothers had to go with them. Roy didn't mind her brothers tagging along, as long as he got to see Lala.

In 1958, Roy had to leave for Germany, but he continued to write Lala and send her pictures. Each picture that he sent would say, "To my one and only. With love and respect, Roy."

On June 7, 1959, while on leave from Germany, Roy married his "One and Only," Hilaria Coy.

WITH THE GREEN Berets heavily on his mind, Roy set out to become the best of the best. The Green Berets are commonly referred to as the Army's Special Forces. They are highly skilled operators, trainers and teachers. They are, indeed, the best of the best, and Roy was out to prove that he could be a part of this elite group of men.

Right before Roy's first tour in Vietnam, Lala gave Roy a medallion for him to wear. As Catholics, they believed in praying to the saints for intercession. Lala pinned a St. Christopher medal on Roy and prayed for his safe return.

November 20, 1965, Fort Bragg, North Carolina. Lala pins Roy with a St. Christopher Medal. St. Christopher is the Patron Saint of Travel.

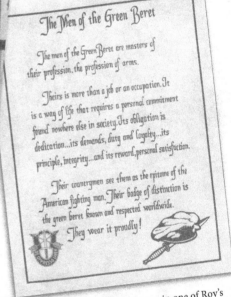

The Men of the Green Beret

The men of the Green Beret are masters of their profession, the profession of arms.

Theirs is more than a job or an occupation. It is a way of life that requires a personal commitment found nowhere else in society. Its obligation is dedication...its demands, duty and loyalty...its principle, integrity...and its reward, personal satisfaction.

Their countrymen see them as the epitome of the American fighting man. Their badge of distinction is the green beret known and respected worldwide. They wear it proudly!

This creed was found tucked away in one of Roy's scrapbooks. He proudly wore the Green Beret.

IN THE ARMY, Roy did two tours in Vietnam. During his first tour, he stepped on a land mine. The shock of the blast injured him so severely doctors said he was paralyzed. The explosion jolted his brain so violently that he wasn't expected to regain his senses, either.

Because of his injuries, he had to be flown to Brooke Army Medical Center in San Antonio, Texas. When he finally awoke, after days of being unconscious, the doctors told him that he would never walk again. He was, indeed, paralyzed from the waist down. He did not want to believe what the doctors were telling him. He wanted to prove them wrong.

During his stay, Roy's wife would visit him often, along with his brother Roger. Lala would bring him sandwiches from home as a special treat. However, Roy's hospital buddies would take his food to trick him. After weeks of this, Roy started asking Lala to put jalapeños in the sandwiches. The next time one of Roy's hospital buddies took a bite out of his sandwich, they got a fiery surprise. Roy did this to teach them a lesson: Don't take things that don't belong to you!

ROY'S RECOVERY WAS a long process. The staff at the hospital believed that he would never walk again, so their therapy was geared toward getting him ready to survive life without the use of his legs. Roy didn't like that, so he took his therapy into his own hands. Every night, he would drag himself out of bed and try to pull himself up against the wall in his hospital room. His roommates would make bets on whether he could do it. Roy did this type of self-therapy without the hospital staff or doctors knowing. After ten months of pure determination and hard work, Roy proved all of the doctors wrong and walked out of that hospital. His perseverance had paid off. He believed that he could do it, and he achieved it. Two years later, Roy trained and qualified to become the best of the best in the Army. He became a Green Beret.

Roy, before he earned the title Green Beret.

THE GREEN BERETS are the elite of the elite, as Roy always said. The qualifications, training and endurance are rigorous. Everything a Green Beret goes through in order to be the best of the best is tough, rugged and draining. Not only is it physically challenging, but it is mentally exhausting as well. Roy secured the distinction of being a Green Beret because he put his mind to it. Who would have ever thought that this son of a sharecropper and grade-school dropout would become part of such an elite group? If you really stop to think about it, how could this man who dropped out of school in the eighth grade study, train, and qualify for this group? How could someone qualify for the Green

Berets who had been told just a year previous that he'd never even walk again — that he'd be paralyzed from the waist down? How could someone who lived his life in physical pain endure the hardcore, labor-intensive training of the Special Forces? His faith, determination and positive attitude played an important role in him achieving his dream.

A moment of distinction for Roy as he proudly wears the Green Beret.

This is one of the actual medallions that Roy wore around his neck. Before he passed away, he gave it to his daughter, Yvette. In gratitude for St. Michael's protection over her father, she named her firstborn son after him —Ryan Michael Garcia. St. Michael has a special place in their hearts.

ON MAY 2, 1968, Roy, or Tango Mike Mike, was in Vietnam for a second time. He was in the jungles of Cambodia attending a church service when he overheard someone on a nearby radio calling in air strikes saying, "Get us out of here!" When Tango Mike Mike heard this call for help, without thinking twice, he quickly grabbed his bowie knife and a medic's bag. He made the sign of the cross and kissed his St. Michael medallion. St. Michael is the patron saint of paratroopers. Now that he was a Green Beret, Roy wore this medallion, too. Roy's devotion to his religion is what got him through his battles in life. He never wavered in his faith.

WITHOUT HESITATION, ROY voluntarily boarded a waiting helicopter. Roy went on this mission because he wanted to, not because he had to or because he was ordered to go. He wanted to go and save his buddies' lives.

Once the helicopter landed in the jungles of Vietnam, Roy jumped out and made it about 100 yards before he was hit by enemy fire. The blast from the gunfire knocked him back, but he got up. He made his way to the team of US soldiers who'd been pinned down by enemy fire and gave them medical care. He also formed a defense and rescue area and called in air strikes. His mission was to save his buddies and bring back classified documents that one of his comrades had. Despite being hit several times by gunshots, grenades and shrapnel, Tango Mike Mike spent six hours in the jungle of Cambodia that day fighting the enemy soldiers. Roy refused to abandon his efforts and would not leave until every man was out of harm's way.

Ultimately, he saved the lives of eight men. On board the helicopter were also several enemy soldiers. Roy later said, "I didn't want to leave anyone behind."

Roy had been clubbed, stabbed, bayoneted, shot and left for dead. His medical reports showed that he had sustained more than fifty-seven wounds to his head, face, neck, hands, arms, legs, back and buttocks. He was injured so badly that, when he was finally lifted onto the helicopter, he was holding his intestines in his hands. He was assumed dead because his injuries were so severe. Eventually, he would be placed into a body bag. As the medic was checking him over to confirm that he was indeed dead, Roy mustered enough strength to spit in the medic's face. That was the only way he could tell him that he was not dead: he was alive. Roy spent the next year undergoing several surgeries to repair all of his injuries.

Roy listens attentively as President Ronald Reagan reads the citation that retells Roy's six-hour mission.

ROY RECEIVED FOUR Purple Hearts as well as the Distinguished Service Cross for his duty that day. Years later, he would be recommended for the Medal of Honor, the highest award bestowed in the military for services performed above and beyond the call of duty.

However, he did not receive this award at that time. Even though he had saved the lives of eight men, there were no eyewitnesses who could attest to what Roy had done on May 2, 1968. The men who Roy had saved were sent to other hospitals for recovery, but Roy didn't know it. He thought they had died. Twelve years later, an eyewitness finally came forward and wrote a ten-page account of what had happened that day. The eyewitness' name was Brian O'Connor.

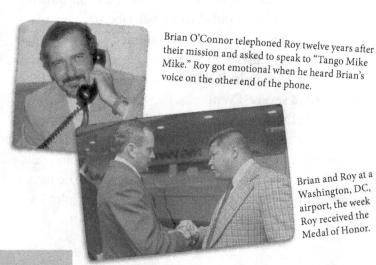

Brian O'Connor telephoned Roy twelve years after their mission and asked to speak to "Tango Mike Mike." Roy got emotional when he heard Brian's voice on the other end of the phone.

Brian and Roy at a Washington, DC, airport, the week Roy received the Medal of Honor.

The crowd numbered several thousand in the center courtyard of the Pentagon.

(Left to right) Denise, Yvette, Noel and Lala at the Medal of Honor Ceremony in Washington, DC. (February 24, 1981)

ON FEBRUARY 24, 1981, thirteen years after his 1968 mission in Vietnam, President Ronald Reagan awarded Master Sergeant Roy P. Benavidez the Medal of Honor. Departing from tradition, Reagan personally read Roy's citation before a crowd of thousands at the Pentagon in Washington, DC. Forty-one members of Roy's family were present to witness this momentous occasion. Before the President draped the medal around Roy's neck, he ended with these words, "A nation grateful to you, and to all of your comrades living and dead, awards you its highest symbol of gratitude for service above and beyond the call of duty, the Congressional Medal of Honor."

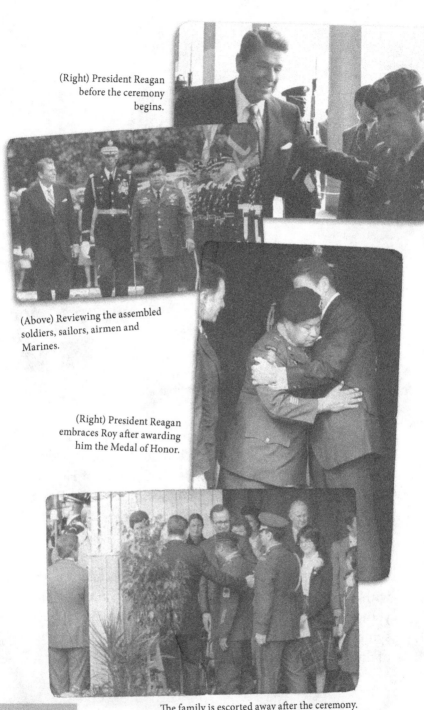

(Right) President Reagan before the ceremony begins.

(Above) Reviewing the assembled soldiers, sailors, airmen and Marines.

(Right) President Reagan embraces Roy after awarding him the Medal of Honor.

The family is escorted away after the ceremony.

Roy and his family on the steps of the White House.

AFTER ROY RECEIVED the medal, he traveled all over the world, speaking at schools, civic organizations, military institutes and Veterans hospitals. His mission was to motivate people to be the best that they could be. He wanted

Roy made it his mission to inspire students to stay in school and get an education.

everyone to know that, although he was deemed a hero, the heroes were the ones who never came home.

In his speeches, Roy talked about coming from a humble background where he had to work to get what he wanted. He spoke about helping his family out in times of need and overcoming a bad attitude about life, people and school to be the best that he could be. He talked about his faith and always putting God first in life. When he spoke to kids in schools, he ended his talks by urging them to stay out of gangs, stay off of drugs and continue their education. He wanted kids to never take things for granted — especially their parents, because he knew what it was like to not have his. He reinforced how a positive attitude will get you farther than ability. Since he was a grade-school dropout, he did not have a formal education. He educated himself by learning from others and by reading books. The more he read, the more he learned. Roy talked about never giving up, no matter what your circumstances in life.

Roy loved to visit his brothers-in-arms. Here he is visiting a VA Hospital during the Christmas season. (December 28, 1981)

ROY BENAVIDEZ PASSED away on November 29, 1998, at 1:33 pm in San Antonio, Texas, at Brooke Army Medical Center, due to complications of diabetes. His family was by his side. On December 4, 1998, he was buried at Fort Sam Houston National Cemetery in San Antonio, with full military honors. Hundreds of people were there to pay their final respects to a man who had given so much in his lifetime. He was only sixty-three years old.

ROY'S FAMILY

ROY'S WIFE, LALA, and their three children — Denise Benavidez Prochazka, Yvette Benavidez Garcia and Noel Benavidez — all live in El Campo, Texas, with their families.

In all, Roy and Lala have eight grandchildren. They have seven grandsons and one granddaughter: Ben, Andrew, Matthew, Joe, Ryan, Jordan, Nicholas and Morgan.

(Right) Hilaria Coy Benavidez, Roy's wife. Roy affectionately called his wife "Lala."

(Above) The Benavidez Family, 1974.

(Left) Yvette Benavidez Garcia and family (Morgan, Ren and Ryan).

(Below) Denise Benavidez Prochazka and Stan.

(Above) Noel Benavidez and family (Matthew, Nicholas, Andrea and Jordan).

(Below) Andrew, Ben and Joe Prochazka.

SINCE HIS PASSING, Roy has received numerous awards posthumously. Many military and civic institutions now bear his name: The Roy P. Benavidez National Guard Armory in El Campo, Texas; a monument in Cuero, Texas; a conference room at West Point; an Army Training Center in North Carolina; a Navy Cargo Ship christened the USNS *Benavidez*; a Community Park in Colorado; two elementary schools (in Houston, Texas, and San Antonio, Texas). In addition he has been the subject of several sculptures, four books and a Hasbro G.I. Joe Action Figure, just to name a few. Today, "Tango Mike Mike" is used in the military as part of their radio training. Soldiers are taught to use the call sign whenever there is trouble, or dire circumstances. Furthermore, if a firefight is going bad or courage needs to be summoned, a soldier will call out:

(Above) The USNS *Benavidez*, currently docked in Bremerton, Washington.

Tango Mike Mike
Tango Mike Mike

Roy's call sign.

(Right) Limited Edition Roy P. Benavidez G.I. Joe Action Figure.

ROY WAS ALWAYS asked, "If you had to do it all over again, would you risk your life to save your buddies?" His answer was always this:

"There will never be enough paper to print the money or enough gold in Fort Knox for me to have, to keep me from doing what I did. I'm proud to be an American and even prouder that I earned the privilege to wear the Green Beret. I live by the motto: Duty, Honor, Country."

CPSIA information can be obtained
at www.ICGtesting.com
Printed in the USA
LVHW091011070321
680749LV00001BA/3/J